CW01512946

Original title:

Brassy Tufts Among the Wizard Yaw

Author: Paulina Pähkel

ISBN HARDBACK: 978-1-80562-646-6

ISBN PAPERBACK: 978-1-80564-167-4

# Sorcerous Highlights on Dreamy Paths

In the twilight's gentle glow,
Whispers of magic softly flow.
Stars above in quiet spark,
Guiding dreams through the dark.

With every footstep, shadows dance,
In this realm of chance and glance.
Colors swirl in twilight's embrace,
Leaving echoes of a trace.

Winds of fortune linger near,
Carrying laughter, love, and cheer.
Each moment a spell untold,
In the heart of paths so bold.

Crickets sing a sweet refrain,
As the night begins to wane.
The moon hangs low, a silver crest,
In this world, we feel so blessed.

Embers fade with dawn's first light,
Yet the magic will ignite.
With the sun, new tales will spin,
As the day begins again.

# Shimmering Canopies Over Mystical Waters

Beneath the leaves, a secret glows,
Where the river of wonder flows.
Ripples dance with a gentle sigh,
Underneath the painted sky.

Light filters through the emerald shade,
Casting spells in the glade.
Each droplet sings of tales anew,
In a world where dreams come true.

Fishes leap with laughter bright,
As the day slips into night.
Reflections whisper ancient lore,
Of futures waiting at the shore.

A chorus of frogs begins to croon,
As stars awaken, bright and strewn.
In this tranquil, enchanted place,
Nature shares her tender grace.

The waters weave a shimmering thread,
Through the stories, brightly spread.
With each wave, a dream takes flight,
Guided by the soft moonlight.

# Vibrant Twists in the Land of the Fae

In realms where the wildflowers leap,
The whispers of faeries softly creep.
Petals glisten, colors collude,
A tapestry of sparkling mood.

Mushrooms dance on surfaces bold,
Secrets of the forest told.
With a twist, the breezes play,
Leading wanderers on their way.

Light flutters in a playful scene,
Where shadows murmur, bright and keen.
Butterflies flutter in vibrant hue,
Each moment feels like something new.

Grounded in magic, lost in a waltz,
Where reality, like a prism, halts.
Here, the air is thick with dreams,
In the land of fae, nothing's as it seems.

Colors swirl in spiraled delight,
As the heart takes flight at night.
In laughter's echo, spirits find
The joyful dance of heart and mind.

## Glimmering Greens Underneath Ancient Boughs


Underneath these ancient trees,
Whispers ride on the gentle breeze.
Roots entwined in tales of yore,
Guarding secrets, dreams, and more.

The sunlight filters, a golden stream,
Weaving through leaves like a waking dream.
A carpet of moss, so lush and deep,
Holds the memories that we keep.

Squirrels chatter, play in the height,
In their games of shadow and light.
Every branch a story to tell,
Of enchantment in this tranquil spell.

The rustle of leaves, a symphony sweet,
Guides the traveler on dancing feet.
Nature hums a soothing song,
In this haven where we belong.

Glimmers of hope in each diamond dew,
A promise of magic, ever true.
With each breath, the heart's embrace,
Time stands still in this sacred place.

# Mystic Folly in the Heart of Enchantment

In shadows where the secrets lie,
Whispers of magic flit and fly.
With every rustle, a tale unfolds,
Of enchantments new and legends old.

Emerald glades with shimmering light,
Hidden paths in the depths of night.
Every creature knows its role,
In this dance of heart and soul.

A flicker of fate in the twilight haze,
Moonlit journeys through starlit maze.
The air thick with dreams and sighs,
As the world beneath the enchantment lies.

Beware the folly of those who seek,
In mystery's hold, the fragile and weak.
For the heart of magic is wild and free,
Boundless as waves of the endless sea.

So walk with grace and trust your mind,
For the truth in the shadows is hard to find.
In the mystic realm where spirits play,
Folly and wisdom dance night and day.

# Lush Highlights Beneath a Spellbound Moon

In silken nights when the stars align,
The moon casts spells, a glow divine.
Lush gardens gleam in mystic light,
Veils of magic weave the night.

Petals whisper secrets rare,
In fragrant breezes, splendor's lair.
Beauty blooms as wishes glide,
And dreams take root where hope resides.

With every breath, enchantments rise,
Underneath vast, twinkling skies.
A serenade of nightingale,
Echoes through the shadowed vale.

Glimmers dance on the dewy leaves,
As ancient magic gently weaves.
In the tapestry of twilight's sigh,
The heart of nature can never die.

Beneath the spellbound moon's embrace,
Lush highlights whisper of grace.
In the stillness, all feels right,
As the world drifts into the night.

## Celestial Whispers Adrift in Brilliance

In the hush of dusk, the cosmos hums,
A chorus of love as starlight comes.
Celestial whispers drift on air,
Tales of wonders beyond compare.

Silver streams in the midnight glow,
Guide the dreamers where they wish to go.
With every twinkle, a heart's delight,
Beneath the vast, eternal night.

Galaxies swirl in a dance so grand,
Threads of fate woven by unseen hand.
Through the stillness, magic flows,
In cosmic currents, the universe grows.

Each moment a spark, a chance to find,
The beauty obscured in fleeting time.
For beneath the starlit expanse we roam,
Whispers lead us back to home.

As dreams take flight on luminous beams,
Celestial depths fulfill our dreams.
In the brilliance of night, our spirits soar,
On the whispers of stars, forevermore.

## Dappled Hues in a Spellbound Garden

In the garden where shadows play,
Colors whisper, bright and gay.
Every petal glistens, a wondrous sight,
In the dappled glow of morning light.

A path woven with lavender dreams,
Flowing through crystalline streams.
Butterflies flutter with tales to tell,
In this enchanted, shimmering spell.

Trees arching like guardians tall,
Listening closely to nature's call.
A breeze sings softly, a tender tune,
Beneath the watchful eye of the moon.

With secrets hidden in every nook,
Magic lingers in every look.
This garden whispers of ancient lore,
Welcoming all who seek to explore.

## Luminous Flora That Dance with Magic

Beneath the starlit, velvet sky,
Luminous blooms flutter and fly.
They twirl and sway in a joyful trance,
Each petal a spell, each leaf a chance.

In midnight's glow, they softly hum,
A melody sweet, eternally spun.
With joy they beckon, inviting all,
To join their circle—come, heed the call!

Glistening dewdrops catch the light,
Turning dreamers into sprites.
They dance in rhythms, wild and free,
In this world of fantasies.

Every fragrance, a story unfolds,
Transcending the silence, breaking the molds.
These flowers of wonder, steeped in delight,
Hold the spark of magic, pure and bright.

## Enchanted Vines and Their Secrets

Winding tales in the moon's embrace,
Enchanted vines weave through time and space.
Whispers of secrets, soft and low,
In every curl, their mysteries grow.

They clamber high, to the heavens they climb,
Each tendril a portal, a step into rhyme.
With every twist, they silently weave,
The stories of hearts that dared to believe.

Through silken threads of emerald grace,
They dance in shadows, a gentle chase.
In their green embrace, dreams come alive,
In the heart of the garden, where magics thrive.

With every bloom, their wisdom shared,
In the rustling leaves, the wise have dared.
These vines, they summon the fae of old,
In their tender grasp, they silently hold.

# Resplendent Foliage in the Eye of the Wizard

Glistening leaves painted with hues,
A wizard's gaze upon the views.
Resplendent foliage whispers their might,
Draped in the colors of day and night.

In the forest, ancient and grand,
Nature's canvas, a painter's hand.
Each leafy crown crowned with fate,
A secret waltz, alluring and late.

With emerald dreams, the branches sway,
In a chorus of green, where shadows play.
Guardians of tales in the twilight's lore,
In the wizard's eye, they forever soar.

Rustling softly with wisdom they share,
In the heart of magic, beyond all care.
These leaves of destiny, vibrant and free,
In the wizard's realm, forever shall be.

# Radiant Locks in the Wizard's Realm

In a chamber cathedrals weave,
Locks of gold and silver gleam,
Whispers float like spells at eve,
Crafting dreams within a dream.

Potions bubble, colors dance,
Mystic mirrors catch the light,
Every strand a tale of chance,
Woven whispers take to flight.

A wand in hand, a flick, a swirl,
A flash of hues, the air ignites,
Masterpieces begin to twirl,
Dancing shadows, starry nights.

In this realm where wonders bloom,
Radiance reigns in every thread,
From the depths of twilight's loom,
Strands of legend, softly spread.

With each thread, a secret spun,
In the magic, hearts unite,
Underneath the watchful sun,
The radiant locks ignite the night.

# Chromatic Whispers in the Twilight

When evening takes a gentle sigh,
The colors paint the sky anew,
From azure drops to crimson high,
Every shade a song, a cue.

In the hush, the breezes sing,
Chromatic whispers fill the air,
Echoing what twilight brings,
Secrets shared without a care.

Leaves aflame, like embers glow,
Softly rustling, tales untold,
In their dance, the colors flow,
A tapestry of dreams unfold.

Magic lingers in the dusk,
Fragrant spells on winds of night,
Through the shadows, dreams we trust,
From the dark emerges light.

And in this time of gentle grace,
Colors whisper, shadows play,
In the twilight's warm embrace,
Hope and magic find their way.

# Ethereal Flares from Arcane Heights

From the peaks where wizards dwell,
Flares of magic rise and soar,
Casting light like whispered spells,
Unlocking worlds forevermore.

Starlit paths and ancient runes,
Ethereal visions come alive,
In the night, the spirit tunes,
Awakening what dreams contrive.

Echoes of the yesteryear,
Dance in light and shadow's grace,
Through the flares, the past is near,
Glowing softly, time's embrace.

Mystic songs in frosty air,
Guide the way to hidden lands,
Every flare a silent prayer,
Written in the sorcerer's hands.

In the skies where secrets twine,
Arcane heights begin to shine,
With each flare, the heart aligns,
Unveiling marvels, pure divine.

## Vivid Hues in an Otherworldly Grove

In the grove where blossoms sway,
Vivid hues weave tales of old,
Every petal on display,
In a world of magic bold.

Whispers of the fae entwined,
Painting dreams upon the air,
Colors dance, their magic blind,
In the twilight, beyond compare.

Mushrooms glow like lanterns bright,
Illuminating paths below,
Guiding creatures of the night,
Through enchanting tales they flow.

In this grove, the heartbeats sing,
Vivid shades of joy and pain,
From the fables, flowers spring,
In each hue, a drop of rain.

As the night unfolds its arms,
Magic lingers, breathes and grows,
In this otherworldly charms,
Vivid hues forever glows.

# Shimmering Locks of the Arcane Wind

In twilight's hush, the whispers fly,
Through trees that sway, beneath the sky.
With every gust, the secrets weave,
The tales of magic, soft to believe.

Locks of silver, golden threads,
Dance in dreams where time now treads.
A breeze that hums of ancient lore,
Guides those who seek for something more.

In shadows cast, the enchantments glow,
Beneath the moon, the soft winds blow.
With every strand, the night unfolds,
A tapestry of stories told.

From distant realms beyond the sight,
The arcane breath brings forth the light.
We gather treasures, lost, yet found,
In shimmering locks, our hearts are bound.

So listen close, the night shall sing,
Of all the wonders that dreams can bring.
In every flicker, charm and grace,
The arcane wind's embrace, our place.

## Illuminated Patches in the Faery Grove

Amidst the woods, where shadows play,
The faery lights come out to stay.
Each glowing patch, a magic spark,
Illuminates the paths so dark.

Upon the leaves, a soft embrace,
The whispered songs of hidden space.
In circles drawn beneath the trees,
Awakening the ancient breeze.

With laughter ringing like a bell,
The faeries weave their charming spell.
In twinkling hues, they dance and glide,
In every moment, dreams abide.

As twilight spills its golden ink,
The magic births in shades to think.
Beneath the moon's enchanted gaze,
The faery grove ignites the haze.

In light's embrace, the spirits twine,
Creating bonds through stars that shine.
In every corner, wonder grows,
In illuminated patches, the magic flows.

# Dazzling Strands in the Realm of Illusions

In realms unseen, where visions play,
The dazzling strands break night from day.
With colors bright, the fables spin,
In threads of gold, the dreams begin.

Through misty veils, illusions bloom,
In every corner, whispers loom.
A dance of light, the hearts shall chase,
Each glinting thread, a fleeting grace.

Let not the shadows dim the quest,
For in each strand, the truth is dressed.
In shimmering worlds, the mind can soar,
With every glimpse, we seek for more.

As laughter echoes in the air,
The realm of dreams, beyond compare.
In dazzling strands, we're intertwined,
The magic's pulse in souls aligned.

So wander forth, with hope alight,
Embrace the realms, both dark and bright.
In every illusion, a story starts,
Dazzling strands entwined in hearts.

# Glittering Blossoms in the Hearth of Spells

In gardens old, where blossoms grow,
The magic hums in every row.
With petals bright, they weave their fate,
In the hearth of spells, they gather weight.

Amidst the blooms, the whispers sigh,
Of tales long lost, beneath the sky.
With gentle hands, the sorcerers tend,
To each bright bud, the spells they send.

In twilight's glow, the colors blend,
In every branch, the secrets bend.
With glittering dreams, the night ignites,
The secret lore of heart's delights.

For every blossom holds a rhyme,
Of wishes made and endless time.
In the magic's cradle, life is spun,
A nursery of spells, the dance begun.

So linger here, where dreams are sown,
In glittering blossoms, the magic's grown.
In the hearth where wonders dwell,
A tale unfolds, we weave, we tell.

# Enchanted Petals in a Wistful Breeze

In the garden where dreams take flight,
Petals dance in the soft moonlight.
Whispers of magic flutter and sway,
Carrying wishes that drift away.

Across the fields, a gentle sigh,
Nature's melody makes hearts fly.
Each bloom twirls like a spun gold thread,
In the silence, old secrets are spread.

With colors bright, they tell their tales,
Of distant lands and forgotten trails.
A breeze enchants the night so still,
Awakening wonders that hearts fulfill.

Underneath the starry sky's tune,
Dew-kissed petals hum to the moon.
In twilight's embrace, all seems at peace,
As the world finds gentle release.

When morning breaks with a silken glow,
The petals rest, yet still they know.
In every flutter, a wish persists,
In enchanted dreams, our hearts coexist.

## Gemlike Fronds in the Glow of Wonder

In the forest where sunlight streams,
Gemlike fronds glisten with hidden dreams.
Each leaf a gem, so rich and rare,
Crafted by time with delicate care.

Mists curl softly, weaving delight,
Kissing each fern in the morning light.
Their emerald whispers, secrets unfold,
Stories of magic, timeless, untold.

As shadows linger and branches sway,
The fronds beckon all to come play.
With every rustle, a tale spun anew,
In the heart of the woods where wonders accrue.

Beneath the boughs, where the fairies glean,
Life dances wildly, elusive yet keen.
The glow of wonder, a cherished embrace,
In the hush of the forest, a sacred place.

When twilight drapes the trees in gold,
The gemlike fronds their stories hold.
In the quietude, magic shall roam,
Amongst the wonders that call it home.

# Brilliance Amongst Shadows of the Arcana

In the depths where shadows quietly dwell,
A brilliance glimmers, casting its spell.
Secrets of arcana, ancient and wise,
Unravel before us like stars in the skies.

With every flicker, hope ignites flame,
Illuminating paths, inviting the same.
The whispers of fire in a darkened room,
Transforming the silence, dispelling the gloom.

An ethereal dance of light and dark,
Fragments of wisdom, each ember a spark.
Through the mist, a figure in flight,
Carrying stories woven in night.

As shadows gather, a symphony swells,
Echoes of longing, the heart gently swells.
In the embrace of the twilight's grace,
Brilliance amidst shadows finds its place.

In every corner where light intertwines,
Magic persists in the paths it designs.
United in shadows, we patiently wait,
For the brilliance of arcana to open the gate.

# Whispered Secrets in the Heart of the Forest

In the heart of the forest, secrets reside,
Whispers of voices that time cannot hide.
The rustle of leaves, a gentle refrain,
Echoes of laughter, love mingled with pain.

Beneath ancient oaks, where shadows entwine,
The spirit of nature begins to align.
Every creature, a story to share,
In the quilted silence, magic is rare.

Moss-covered paths lead to wonders untold,
With each new step, the mysteries unfold.
Breezes carry tales of enchantment alive,
In a magical world where dreams still thrive.

The song of the forest, a timeless delight,
Binds us to nature, both day and night.
In the dense thickets, our souls intertwine,
In whispered secrets, a bond we define.

So wander gently, with heart open wide,
For whispered secrets are spirits that guide.
In the embrace of the trees, we stand free,
In the heart of the forest, wild magic we'll see.

## Wild Vines Amidst Sorcery's Breath

In shadowed groves where wild vines creep,
Mysteries woven, secrets deep.
The whispering leaves in moonlight dance,
Eager to share their ancient chance.

With spells of old in gentle twine,
They cradle dreams, both yours and mine.
A tangle of thoughts, in colors bright,
They weave through the darkness, seeking light.

From roots that touch the earth's embrace,
To blossoms poised in a starry lace,
Each vine a story, rich and rare,
Beneath the spell of midnight air.

So wander through this magic found,
Where nature's whispers weave around.
As sorcery breathes in the starlit night,
The wild vines sway, a wondrous sight.

## Reflective Petals in the Enchanted Air

Soft petals drift on a breeze so fair,
Glowing treasures in the enchanted air.
They catch the light with a silken grace,
Each hue a memory in time and space.

Around them swirls a soft, warm glow,
The secrets of nature begin to flow.
Each breath a promise, tenderly spun,
A dance of petals 'neath the warming sun.

In gardens where dreams in shadows bloom,
Reflective petals dispel the gloom.
With every flutter, a wish takes flight,
A delicate symphony of pure delight.

They whisper tales of love and cheer,
Inviting hearts to draw near.
In this realm where wonders share,
A fragrant promise lingers in the air.

# Fanciful Greens in the Heart of Whimsy

In the heart of whimsy, where laughter grows,
Fanciful greens in a cascade flows.
They shimmer with magic, song, and jest,
A tapestry woven, forever blessed.

With every leaf that dances free,
A giggle rises, like waves at sea.
In meadows lush, where dreams entwine,
The fanciful greens begin to shine.

They cradle the light of a child's grace,
Each playful shadow a warm embrace.
In the tilt of a tree and the swirl of air,
Whimsy's echoes linger everywhere.

So come, dear friend, and chase the breeze,
Among the greens, feel your worries ease.
In this magical realm of playful delight,
The fanciful greens will hold you tight.

## Dauntless Blades in the Forest of Dreams

In the forest of dreams where shadows loom,
Dauntless blades rise, piercing the gloom.
Each edge a promise, sharp and true,
Defying the darkness, breaking through.

They stand like sentinels, proud and tall,
Guardians of secrets in twilight's call.
With every gust of the midnight air,
The dauntless blades sing a song of dare.

Among the trees where the night unfolds,
A magic of courage in their holds.
They carve a path through lingering fears,
Leading the way with laughter and cheers.

In the heart of the woods, where dreams ignite,
Bravery blooms in the still of night.
So heed the call of the forest's embrace,
Let dauntless blades guide you to grace.

# Chromatic Locks in the Sorcerer's Grasp

In the shadows where colors twine,
Secrets whisper through the vine.
A sorcerer weaves with careful hands,
Unlocking dreams in mystical lands.

Rainbow hues in a delicate dance,
Mysteries held in a silken trance.
Each hue reflects a time long lost,
Bound by spells, no matter the cost.

A flick of a wand, a heart's desire,
Unlocking gates to worlds on fire.
With every turn of a chromatic key,
Legends bloom that none can foresee.

As twilight falls, the colors fade,
A magic spell silently laid.
In the realm where shadows grow,
The locks reveal their secrets slow.

Beyond the grasp of mere mortals' sight,
Shimmering locks unveil the night.
In the sorcerer's grasp, all things transform,
Colors alive in a wild storm.

# Enigmatic Greens in the Twilight's Embrace

In the silence of the evening's glow,
Emerald leaves begin to flow.
Enigmas dance in the cool, crisp air,
Whispers of secrets beyond compare.

The twilight deepens, shadows creep,
While ancient guardians quietly sleep.
In the heart of the forest, mysteries thrive,
Colorful stories, vibrant and alive.

Each rustling branch, a tale untold,
Of spirits brave and hearts of gold.
Through tangled paths, the seekers tread,
Chasing dreams where none dare to tread.

In the depths of an emerald haze,
A glimpse of magic through the maze.
With every step, the world unfolds,
Enchantments woven in timeless molds.

The stars awaken, a celestial show,
Lighting the landscape, setting it aglow.
In twilight's embrace, the heart takes flight,
For enigmatic greens dance in the night.

## Shining Hues in Fantastical Haze

In a realm where dreams collide,
Shining hues of magic abide.
Fantastical wonders drift and sway,
Chasing shadows, keeping fears at bay.

A brush of whispers paints the sky,
Where stories bloom and spirits fly.
Colors vibrant in a swirling sea,
Boundless realms of creativity.

Hues of joy and sparks of grace,
Guide the traveler through time and space.
In every corner, mysteries gleam,
Awakening the heart's boldest dream.

Fog dances lightly like a feathered sigh,
Wrapping the world in a delicate lie.
In this haze, all things seem near,
Chasing the echoes of laughter and cheer.

With every heartbeat, the colors shift,
A magical spell that's forever a gift.
In shining hues, we learn to believe,
In a fantastic dream, we dare to weave.

# Mythic Strands Beneath Enchanted Arches

Beneath the arches of ancient lore,
Mythic strands entwine evermore.
In whispered tales and forgotten dreams,
Magic flows in glimmering streams.

The starlit path beckons strong,
As echoes of history sing their song.
Interlaced destinies, woven tight,
Breathe life into the heart of night.

In tangled webs where secrets reside,
The essence of magic cannot hide.
A journey begins with every thread,
Through enchanted arches where few have tread.

The moonlight dances on silvered streams,
Tracing the patterns of woven dreams.
In timeless pursuit of what lies ahead,
Hopes and wishes on stardust are fed.

As dawn approaches, threads intertwine,
Building a bridge, an arc divine.
Through mythic strands, we weave our fate,
Beneath the arches, we celebrate.

# Vivid Plumes in the Land of Enchantment

In meadows bright where shadows weave,
The flowers dance, their colors cleave.
With laughter soft, they paint the air,
A tapestry of joy laid bare.

Through whispering winds, their secrets flow,
In rainbow arcs, their spirits glow.
Each petal holds a tale untold,
Of magic spun in threads of gold.

Beneath the sun's warm, gentle rays,
The vivid hues ignite the days.
In every glance, a spark alights,
Transforming dreams into delights.

The brook nearby sings soft and sweet,
Its murmured notes a rhythmic beat.
As creatures dance in pure delight,
The vivid plumes take radiant flight.

In twilight's hush, a spell is cast,
The vibrant shades hold legends fast.
In shadows deep, where wonders gleam,
The land unfolds its softest dream.

## Luminous Foliage Beneath Starlit Skies

The leaves aglow in moonlit grace,
Reveal a world, a hidden space.
Where whispers weave through branches high,
And secrets float like dust on sighs.

With twinkling lights, the night awakes,
As silence dances, softly breaks.
The twilight hush, a velvet cloak,
Embraces all that dreams invoke.

Each fluttering leaf a story sings,
Of ancient lands and magical things.
In shadows deep, the spirits glide,
Through luminous threads, they joyfully bide.

Glowing orbs in velvet skies,
Guide wandering hearts with gentle sighs.
The stars align, a path reveals,
Of mysteries that time conceals.

In every breeze, the magic swirls,
Among the leaves, the wonder twirls.
Beneath the stars, a dream takes flight,
In luminous foliage, pure delight.

# The Sorcery of Verdant Highlights


In forest deep, where shadows grow,
The verdant hues begin to glow.
A symphony of greens and golds,
Where nature's art, her magic, unfolds.

Each blade of grass, a wand of light,
With whispers soft, they spark the night.
In every corner, life ignites,
As verdant highlights weave their flights.

The branches echo ancient lore,
Of creatures great, and realms before.
In twilight's grasp, the colors blend,
New stories born, as old ones end.

From emerald beds, the wildflowers soar,
Their vibrant crowns, the earth's rapport.
The hidden paths invite the brave,
To dance where dreams and forests wave.

Among the leaves, the magic spills,
In laughter's song and time's sweet thrills.
The sorcery of life abounds,
In verdant highlights, joy resounds.

# Whimsical Tendrils Adrift in Otherworldly Air

In twilight's embrace, the tendrils sway,
Through whimsical realms, they float and play.
With breath of stars, they drift along,
Creating a melody, soft and strong.

They twine through dreams, in colors bright,
In otherworldly air, a dance of light.
Each flicker holds a whisper's charm,
A fleeting touch, a gentle balm.

In flickering shades, the night reveals,
A tapestry of joy it feels.
With every leap, the world ignites,
Through whimsical visions, pure delights.

Adrift like clouds in a realm so rare,
The tendrils weave through scented air.
Among the stars, they twirl and spin,
Inviting all to dance within.

In magical moments, time stands still,
With tendrils twining over hill.
In otherworldly air, we dare
To dream a dream, as light and flair.

# Golden Whispers in the Magic Gale

In twilight's embrace, the shadows dance,
Whispers of dreams float on a chance.
The winds weave tales of magic and fate,
Golden secrets in the night await.

Moonlight glimmers on leaves of gold,
Stories of ancients quietly told.
A flutter, a spark, ignites the air,
Awakens the heart with gentle care.

In the realm where wishes freely soar,
The magic gale sings, forevermore.
With every breath, a spell is spun,
In golden realms, where dreams are won.

Echoes of laughter blend with the breeze,
Nature's symphony, a heart that sees.
As stardust blankets the earth in twine,
The magic gale, a gift divine.

So listen closely to the winds tonight,
For in the whispers lies pure delight.
With every sigh, enchantments reveal,
The golden dreams that the heart can feel.

# Tresses of Amber in Enchanted Breezes

Through fields of wonder, the wild blooms sway,
Tresses of amber in the light of day.
Enchanted breezes carry the sound,
Of laughter and joy that know no bound.

Each petal a story, each fragrance a song,
In this realm of magic, where we belong.
Underneath the sky, painted in hues,
Amber whispers share ancient views.

Beneath canopies where the fairies dwell,
Secrets of nature, they weave a spell.
The rustle of leaves, a soft lullaby,
As the sun slowly bows to the sky.

With every step on the mossy ground,
In each moment, new wonders abound.
Golden locks in the breeze entwine,
Nature's dance, a tale divine.

So tread with care through this sacred space,
Where every breath carries a trace.
Of tresses of amber, so soft and bright,
In enchanted breezes, find pure light.

# Radiant Sprouts Beneath the Sorcerer's Eye

In shadowed glades where the magic sleeps,
Radiant sprouts rise from ancient keeps.
Beneath the gaze of the sorcerer's eye,
Dreams ignite and twinkle in the sky.

Emerald shoots in the softened light,
Awaken the magic that glimmers bright.
With every pulse of the earth's own breath,
Life's vibrant dance defies even death.

A spark of wonder in the verdant shade,
Each seed carries tales of the choices made.
Within the soil, where the mysteries lie,
Hope sprouts forth with a daring sigh.

As twilight descends and shadows blend,
Nature's embrace becomes our friend.
In the hush of night, the whispers call,
Of radiant sprouts that inspire us all.

So gather 'round as the stars align,
To witness the magic that is divine.
Beneath the sorcerer's watchful eye,
The world awakens with each passing sigh.

# Kaleidoscope Fronds in a Mystic Realm

In a realm where colors boldly sway,
Kaleidoscope fronds dance in bright array.
Through pathways woven with light and shade,
Mystic wonders in peace are laid.

Each leaf a canvas, each petal a hue,
Reflecting the dreams of me and you.
With every turn, new stories to tell,
In this magical place where spirits dwell.

The air is thick with a sweet perfume,
As blossoms unfold in their vibrant bloom.
In the heart of the forest, inspiration flows,
Through the kaleidoscope fronds, compassion grows.

Listen closely to the whispers of trees,
They tell of the past, carried by the breeze.
In this mystic realm, where the heart can roam,
The world becomes a vibrant home.

So come, dear wanderer, seek what's true,
In the embrace of the wild, find the new.
For in this kaleidoscope of delight,
Every moment dances in purest light.

# The Dance of Colors on Enchanted Grounds

In the glade where shadows play,
The flowers bloom in bright array.
With whispers soft, they start to sway,
As twilight drapes the end of day.

A tapestry of nature's art,
Each petal holds a beating heart.
With every breeze, they twist and dart,
In harmony, they won't depart.

The moonlight sprinkles silver dust,
Through mist and magic, dance they must.
In every hue, in every gust,
On enchanted grounds, they trust.

Beneath the stars, their secrets bloom,
In secret nooks, where shadows loom.
The air is filled with sweet perfume,
In nature's dance, they find their room.

So take a step, join in the song,
Where colors weave, where spirits throng.
In this enchanted place, you'll belong,
With every beat, the world feels strong.

## Fantastical Flora in a Realm Unspoken

In meadows wild, where dreams are spun,
The flora thrives, an endless run.
With petals bright as morning sun,
In whispers soft, their tales begun.

Each leaf enchanted, secret bound,
In harmony, their voices found.
With colors vivid, all around,
In realms unspoken, magic crowned.

The azure sky, a canvas wide,
Where mystical beings take their stride.
In every nook, the blooms abide,
With fables told, the heart's a guide.

From twilight's grace to dawn's embrace,
In the flora's waltz, we find our place.
With every glance, we feel the grace,
In this fantastical, timeless space.

Invite the wonder, let it soar,
As nature's beauty opens door.
A realm awaits, forevermore,
Where every bloom ignites the lore.

## Celestial Sprouts in a Lush Enigma

Where stardust kisses earthly ground,
Celestial sprouts begin unbound.
In whispers soft, their tales are found,
In lush enigmas, wonders abound.

Each budding life with a spark of light,
Within the shadows, dreams take flight.
In harmony, they gleam so bright,
In every heartbeat, pure delight.

In valleys deep, where secrets hide,
The flora sways at night's soft tide.
Their vibrant hues can't be denied,
A dance of hope and love allied.

With every dawn, the world awakes,
In nature's rhythm, the magic shakes.
With tender roots, the earth remakes,
Celestial dreams that life partakes.

So wander forth, embrace the flow,
In every sprout, let wonder grow.
In lush enigmas, hearts shall glow,
As unity within us shows.

# Verdant Findings in the Embrace of the Unknown

In emerald fields where whispers sigh,
Venturing forth beneath the sky.
With every step, a chance to fly,
In verdant findings, spirits lie.

Each shade of green, a story told,
In hidden paths, the brave and bold.
With nature's heart, the world unfolds,
In the embrace, the mysteries hold.

From leafy canopies, secrets spark,
With playful breezes, leaving mark.
In every corner, light and dark,
In nature's bond, the scepters arc.

A touch of dew, a hint of grace,
As soft as dreams in a serene space.
In every breath, the wild embrace,
Awakening passions we must face.

So take a walk, let worries cease,
In verdant realms, we find our peace.
In nature's arms, our hearts release,
In the unknown, forever increase.

## Crowned by the Glories of Spellbound Strands

Crowned in the moonlight, spun from dreams,
Where whispers of magic dance and gleam.
Each strand a story, woven so tight,
Glories unfurling in the soft twilight.

Stars twinkle softly from ethereal skies,
As spellbound hearts weave their tender ties.
With each flick of wands, a shimmer ignites,
In this realm of wonder, enchantment delights.

Gossamer threads in colors untold,
In patterns of secrets, both brave and bold.
With laughter that echoes through forest glades,
Crowned are the glories that never shall fade.

Voices of ancients, in harmony sing,
Through every fiber, the magic takes wing.
With courage and wisdom laced in the air,
Crowned by the glories, enchantments laid bare.

In twilight's embrace, where stories entwine,
Each thread holds a wish, a destiny fine.
Crowned in the glories that shimmer and sway,
In the tapestry woven, forever we'll stay.

# Threads of Allure in a Mystic Gale

In the whispering winds where secrets sigh,
Threads of allure in the night sky fly.
Dancing with shadows, they twirl and weave,
Concealing the tales that none can perceive.

Beneath the glow of the silvery moon,
Mystic gales hum an age-old tune.
With every gust, a promise ignites,
Threads of enchantment in magical nights.

Each shimmer a memory, sweet and profound,
As time swirls around in a soft, gentle round.
The allure of magic makes mortals believe,
In the threads of the night, there's more to achieve.

With courage entwined through the fabric of chance,
Adventures await in this spellbinding dance.
Threads of allure guide the bold and the wise,
In the heart of the gale, where true magic lies.

So follow the whispers, let them lead you far,
To the edge of the world where wonders are.
In threads of allure, find your own tale,
As hearts intertwine in a mystic gale.

# Luminous Afros in Ancient Rites

Luminous afros in the warm summer glow,
Eddies of laughter, where friendships flow.
Ancient rites whisper through vibrant strands,
Binding the hearts with invisible hands.

In circles of joy, where stories are spun,
Underneath skies where the setting sun.
Dances of light, in colors so bright,
Luminous magic in the softening night.

With every beat of the drum that resounds,
The rhythm of life in ancestral grounds.
Afros adorned in the sun's gentle hues,
Shine with the wisdom of ages, infused.

Celebrations rise with a victorious cheer,
Carried on winds that we all hold dear.
Luminous bonds form in the magic of sights,
Embracing the joys of our ancient rites.

Each lock a beacon, a legacy bold,
Sharing the warmth that the universe holds.
In the heart of the night, as the spirit ignites,
We gather as one in our luminous rites.

# Nature's Splendor in a Woven Wizardry

Nature's splendor, a tapestry bright,
Woven with starlight, both wondrous and light.
Each thread a whisper of secrets untold,
Wizardry dances through valleys of gold.

In the heart of the woods, where magic takes flight,
Colors of autumn paint the world so right.
With each gentle breeze, the trees softly sway,
Nature's own song in a harmonious play.

Delicate flowers in gardens abound,
With petals like treasures beneath the soft ground.
Woven together in patterns divine,
Nature's splendor, a gift most fine.

With echoes of laughter that ring through the trees,
And dreams carried forward on each summer breeze,
In the heart of the forest, a haven we find,
Woven wizardry, where spirits unwind.

So wander the pathways where enchantments glide,
Embrace nature's beauty, let your heart ride.
For in every moment, in all that we see,
Nature's splendor sings a grand tapestry.

# Glints of Brass in Eldritch Breezes

In the shadowed woods, a whisper sings,
Of ancient trees and spectral things.
Where glints of brass in twilight glow,
And secrets dance in the winds that blow.

Wanderers tread on paths of gold,
With tales of wonder and sights untold.
The air is thick with timeless grace,
As shadows shift in their hidden place.

Glimpse the flicker of a distant light,
A promise beckons through the night.
Echoes linger, soft and low,
In the heart of where the dreamers go.

Watch as stars reveal their play,
In patterns spun from night and day.
A symphony of whispers sighs,
Beneath the tapestry of skies.

In every gust, a charm is cast,
From stories woven in the past.
Through glints of brass, the magic weaves,
In the eldritch dance that never leaves.

# Shimmering Curls of Enchantment

In the moonlit grove, a maiden fair,
With shimmering curls, free as the air.
Her laughter flows like a gentle stream,
A melody born of a waking dream.

Around her twirls the magic bright,
A spark in the shadows, a glimmering light.
Each hair a thread of a spell unspun,
In the realm of night where wonders run.

The whispers of fairies, soft and clear,
Guide the lost souls who wander near.
With every step, enchantments rise,
As stardust falls from the velvet skies.

A dance of leaves in the breeze so light,
Reflects the beauty of her spirit's flight.
In twilight's embrace, she weaves her art,
With shimmering curls that captivate the heart.

Through spells of joy and incense sweet,
In twinkling corners, fate does meet.
For every wanderer, a wish takes flight,
In shimmering curls beneath the night.

## Mystical Whorls in Celestial Night

In the depths of night, where silence reigns,
Whispers of magic stir the plains.
Mystical whorls like clouds of dust,
Twirl with the stars, in shadows we trust.

The moon keeps guard with a watchful eye,
As constellations weave and sigh.
A tapestry bright, hung high above,
In the embrace of the night, we feel love.

With echoes of laughter, the night unfolds,
In tales of wonder, adventure bold.
Each twinkling star holds a story dear,
In mystical whorls, the cosmos near.

Ripples of light like a gentle wave,
Chase the mysteries that we crave.
In every glimmer, a secret lies,
Unveiled in the dance of the midnight skies.

Through darkened paths where dreams take flight,
The heart ignites at the edge of night.
Mystical whorls in silence weave,
A spell of magic that we believe.

## The Gilded Tresses of Midnight Magic

In the hush of dusk, a glimmer shines,
With gilded tresses like sunlit vines.
Midnight magic drapes its cloak,
In whispers sweet, the secrets spoke.

A flicker of gold in twilight's embrace,
Befriends the stars in their endless chase.
Each curl a twist of fate's delight,
Guiding dreams through the veil of night.

Her laughter rings like chimes of old,
With stories spun in threads of gold.
In every sigh, a yearning sways,
Through gilded tresses, hope displays.

Around her gather the fireflies' dance,
In swirling patterns of wistful romance.
Their light entwines with her radiant glow,
A moment captured, a treasure to show.

With echoes soft of ancient lore,
The night reveals what we adore.
Through gilded tresses, a pathway gleams,
To midnight magic, and our deepest dreams.

# Spirited Foliage on Forgotten Pathways

In shadows deep, where whispers dwell,
The leaves converse, a secret spell.
In emerald hues, they dance and sway,
On winding paths, they softly play.

The sturdy oaks, their branches high,
Embrace the breeze, and catch the sky.
With every rustle, tales unfold,
Of ancient woods and spirits bold.

The twilight paints a world anew,
While crickets sing their evening rue.
Beneath a bough, the memories creep,
As all the forest dreams in sleep.

From roots to tips, the magic flows,
As silken strands of moonlight glows.
In this realm of fleeting time,
The heart finds peace in whispered rhyme.

So wander forth, young soul of night,
Through foliage wrapped in soft starlight.
For here in dreams, the past stands tall,
In spirited whispers—the call of all.

# Iridescent Vegetation in the Spellbound Glade

In glades where sunlight weaves its thread,
Iridescent hues are delicately spread.
Foliage twirls in a vibrant dance,
Beneath the spell of fate and chance.

The petals shimmer in a gentle breeze,
As laughter echoes through enchanted trees.
A vivid canvas of greens and gold,
With stories untold, waiting to unfold.

Among the petals, fairies play,
Dancing in light, they drift and sway.
To the rhythm of the wild, they sing,
Hearts entwined in the joy they bring.

The brook nearby hums a sweet refrain,
While dragonflies trace the sun's soft stain.
In this verdant realm of dreams, they weave,
A tapestry woven for those who believe.

With every step, feel magic's spark,
In this spellbound glade where wonders embark.
Let nature's colors and sounds collide,
As the heart finds solace, side by side.

# Woven Hues of Light and Shadow

In twilight's web, where light and shade,
Are woven threads, a grand charade.
The world transforms in soft delight,
As day concedes to gentle night.

Trees with bark of muted gray,
Stand sentinel as dusk decays.
Through emerald leaves, the starlight peeks,
While whispered breezes weave soft speaks.

Illuminated glimmers on silver streams,
Reflect the secrets of whispered dreams.
With every ripple and every gleam,
The echoes of shadows call and redeem.

Woven hues that softly blend,
Reveal the beauty that never ends.
In dusk's embrace, the heart discovers,
A world of magic, kisses of lovers.

So tread the pathways, light your way,
In dance with shadows that weave and sway.
For in this realm of twilight's glow,
Woven hues hold love's sacred flow.

## Echoes of the Emerald Grasslands


In fields of green, where wildflowers thrive,
The echoes of life dance, jump, and dive.
A symphony sung by the wind's sweet hand,
Carrying whispers across the land.

Beneath the sky of endless blue,
The grasslands sing—both old and new.
With every breeze, a bewitching call,
The beating heart of nature enthralls.

The sun-kissed blooms, in vibrant array,
Sway with the rhythm of brightening day.
In quiet moments between the swells,
Lies the magic that nature dwells.

In the rustling leaves and sinking light,
The stories awaken, ready to ignite.
With every shadow, a tale is spun,
Of dreams undying, of hope begun.

So wander forth through emerald seas,
Let the whispers guide you with ease.
In the echoes of these grasslands wide,
Find your heart and let it glide.

# The Twisted Brass of Enigmatic Spirits

In shadows deep where whispers dwell,
Twisted brass rings a secret bell.
Spirits dance in a ghostly light,
Veiled in dreams of the starlit night.

A fluttering breeze, tales on the air,
Of ancient joys and forgotten care.
They weave through the fog, a mystical song,
Echoing softly, where shadows belong.

The moon hangs low, a watchful eye,
Guarding secrets of the elusive sky.
With glimmers of silver, they tease and play,
In the twilight's embrace, they gently sway.

What stories lie in the twisted brass?
Of lost, forgotten souls that pass.
Through corridors of time, they seep,
Awakening dreams from the depths of sleep.

So listen close, to the night's sweet tune,
For within the hush, the spirits croon.
Their laughter lingers, a distant chime,
In the twisted brass, we dance with time.

## Captivating Fringes Beneath Wandering Stars

On captivating fringes, where shadows meet,
Beneath wandering stars, our hearts skip a beat.
In the chill of the night, our spirits arise,
Chasing the magic that glimmers and flies.

Every flicker above, tells a tale untold,
Of galaxies swirling, of dreams turned to gold.
With each shooting star, a wish takes flight,
Carried away on the wings of the night.

The cosmos unfurls its tapestry bright,
Weaving desires in whispers of light.
In the echoing silence, our secrets we share,
As constellations spin in celestial air.

A symphony played on the strings of the sky,
Where moonbeams dance and the night owls fly.
In moments like these, we find our true place,
Wrapped in the wonder of time and of space.

So gather your hopes, beneath skies so vast,
Where dreams intertwine, and shadows are cast.
In the heart of this magic, we boldly will dare,
To chase the enchanting, to breathe the rare air.

## Luscious Manes of the Arcane Skies

Luscious manes of the arcane skies,
Flow like rivers where mystery lies.
Each hue a whisper, each strand a vow,
A tapestry painted, a magic somehow.

As the twilight descends, colors take flight,
Emerald greens blend with deep indigo night.
Glimmers of gold streak the velvety gray,
In this cosmic cauldron, dreams glow and sway.

Caught in the strands of celestial hair,
Wonders awaken, float free in the air.
The pull of the galaxies tugs at our hearts,
As we dance with the cosmos, where magic imparts.

Every glance at the sky tells a story anew,
Of legends and fables, both fierce and true.
The whispers of starlight lead us astray,
Yet in their embrace, we'd forever stay.

So let us rejoice in the hues overhead,
In luscious manes where our dreams are spread.
For in these horizons, our spirits are freed,
In the arcane skies, we'll forever heed.

## Tresses Wrought with Myths and Marvels

Tresses wrought with myths and marvels rare,
Cascading down like whispers in air.
Each lock a legend, each curl a tale,
Of heroes and fables that never grow stale.

In moonlit gardens where secrets reside,
Strands shimmer softly, with gods as our guide.
Glimmers of laughter, stories unfold,
In the warmth of the night, magic behold.

With woven knots of ancient delight,
We embrace the shadows, welcoming light.
For in every tress lies a bond intertwined,
Of dreams once forgotten and wishes aligned.

So let your heart dance in this silken embrace,
Of myths and marvels, a timeless grace.
With whispers of magic, let us inspire,
The tresses that twinkle, aglow with desire.

And as dawn beckons, let stories anew,
Be shaped by the light, by love ever true.
For in every tress lies a world to explore,
Wrought with the magic that we all adore.

# Vibrant Blades Amongst the Sorcerous Wilds

In the heart of the wood, where shadows play,
Vibrant blades of grass dance in the fray.
Whispers of magic float through the air,
Wilds of wonder that beckon and dare.

Underneath boughs of a twilight hue,
Glowing petals bloom, kissed by the dew.
Secrets are woven by nature's own hand,
In this realm so strange, so quietly grand.

Faint echoes of laughter, a spellbinding tune,
Spilling like starlight beneath the croon.
Fairies and sprites flit with joy in their hearts,
Creating enchantments with whimsical arts.

Mossy stones guard the trails of the night,
While creatures both shy and bold take flight.
Each rustle and murmur a story untold,
Of vibrant blades dancing, both fearless and bold.

## Celestial Greens Amid Arcane Echoes

In the glades where moonlight softly spills,
Celestial greens climb the ancient hills.
Arcane echoes hum in the gentle breeze,
A haunting lullaby, where dreams find ease.

Nature's quill writes on parchment of time,
With ink made of starlight, all flowing in rhyme.
Each leaf sings a tale from the whispers of yore,
As secrets of old awaken once more.

Beneath the rich canopy, shadows entwine,
Promising magic, a world so divine.
With every step deeper into the dream,
The heart beats in rhythm, a soft, steady theme.

From roots hidden deep, to branches that sway,
Celestial wonders emerge in their play.
With footfalls as light as a whispering sigh,
The wild calls the seekers, to soar and to fly.

### Glistening Strays in the Hallowed Woods

Through hallowed woods where the shallows gleam,
Glistening strays wander, lost in their dream.
Each path twists and turns with secrets untold,
A world brimming bright with adventure and bold.

In pools of reflected enchantments, they pause,
To marvel at wonders with wide-eyed applause.
Twinkling stars hide beneath leafy crowns,
As shadows of night dance with soft, silken frowns.

A rustling sentience lingers so near,
While ancient trees murmur in voices sincere.
This realm, full of magic, ignites the heart's flame,
As glistening strays continue their game.

Amidst the thick mist that blankets the path,
Joy springs eternal, a sweet aftermath.
The pulse of the woods thrums steady and clear,
In this sanctuary, nothing to fear.

# Ethereal Threads in a Dreamer's Realm

In the tapestry woven of dreams and of light,
Ethereal threads entwine in the night.
Whispers of wishes like clouds drift and sway,
Dancing on breezes that softly convey.

Awash in the glow of shimmering stars,
Where reality mingles with stories from Mars.
A flicker of fate stirs the dust of the day,
As dreamers embark on their magical way.

Each step leaves a trace, a footprint of truth,
A journey of heart, a return to lost youth.
In this realm of illusion, so vivid, so warm,
The mind finds its harvest in the silence of charm.

With laughter like petals, they sprinkle the air,
In a symphony played by the bold and the rare.
Ethereal visions ignite in the dark,
Awakening wonders that endlessly spark.

## Iridescent Whiskers of Grassy Halos


Beneath the moon's soft, silver glow,
Whiskers dance where the wild winds blow.
Emerald threads in night's embrace,
Twinkling softly, full of grace.

Each blade a brush, a stroke of light,
Painting shadows, the stars ignite.
A symphony woven in whispers' thread,
In this realm where dreams are fed.

Glimmers flicker, a secret's tease,
Magic stirs on a gentle breeze.
Iridescent halos spin and sway,
In the heart of the night's ballet.

Through the chaos of nightly air,
The grassy realms hide secrets rare.
With each soft step, the whispers rise,
A tapestry spun from starlit sighs.

So lay your heart on this verdant bed,
Where the night sings stories, softly spread.
Iridescent whisks in dance, beguile,
Enchanting all with a mystical smile.

# Dazzling Hues Beneath a Magician's Canvas

Underneath the magician's sway,
Colors leap and twist in play.
Crimson flashes, enchanted bright,
Bathe the world in joyful light.

Canvas stretched 'neath the starlit dome,
Painted worlds, a wondrous home.
Every stroke a spark of fate,
Dancing realms that fascinate.

With a flick, a twist, and turn,
The hearts of all begin to yearn.
Golden beams in layers unspool,
Mystic shadows, a painter's tool.

Lavender dreams swirl in the air,
Caught between with elegance rare.
A dazzling show for those who see,
The magic sewn with pure esprit.

Within the hues, tales intertwine,
Stories whispered in every line.
Beneath the paint, wonders enfold,
In the magician's hands, dreams told.

# Whispering Stems in a Celestial Choir

Among the blooms with petals wide,
Whispering stems, in shadows hide.
A choir sings from roots so deep,
In harmony, the earth does keep.

Celestial notes tumble and soar,
Tales of twilight forever more.
In every rustle, secrets roam,
A world of voices feels like home.

Beneath the stars, the grass does sway,
In the cool embrace of night and play.
Symphony sweet, the breeze's sigh,
I whisper back to the starry sky.

Echoes twine through the moonlit glades,
A gentle tune that never fades.
Each little stem, a story shared,
In twilight's breath, they are prepared.

So heed the whispers, soft and clear,
In the choir's warmth, you'll find no fear.
For in the night, with starlight's grace,
The garden sings, a sacred space.

# Glowing Greens in the Tapestry of Night

In the tapestry of endless night,
Glowing greens flicker, pure delight.
Emerald dreams that softly gleam,
Woven threads, like a midnight stream.

Moonlit foliage dances, alive,
Where shadows whisper and creatures thrive.
In every corner, secrets bloom,
With verdant flames dispelling gloom.

Crickets hum a symphony sweet,
Nature's choir swells at our feet.
A lanterned glow upon the grass,
Guiding steps as you gently pass.

Rustling leaves tell tales untold,
In the night's embrace, brave and bold.
Each glowing green, a magic spark,
Illuminates the paths so dark.

So wander through this verdant night,
Find solace in the glowing light.
For in this world, with dreams alight,
Glowing greens weave tales of delight.

# Sunlit Fronds in the Whispering Mist

Gentle light through emerald leaves,
Whispers dance on morning's breath.
Fronds unfurl where shadows weave,
Nature sings of life, of death.

Misty tapestries unfold,
Color soft against the gray.
Secrets of the dawn retold,
In the hush of break of day.

Brightened paths where fairies tread,
Glistening dew in sun's embrace.
Each step, stories gently thread,
Magic lives in every space.

Beneath the boughs, a silent cheer,
Rhythms of the earth resound.
In every heartbeat, crystal clear,
Life's enigma knows no bound.

Echoes linger in the air,
As the day begins to rise.
Beauty wraps the world in care,
Sunlit fronds, a sweet surprise.

# Lush Hues Beneath a Moonlit Arc

In shadows cast by silver glow,
Colors pulse on hushed terrain.
Whispers soft as breezes blow,
Dreams emerge, unloosed from chain.

Night's embrace ignites the sky,
Emerald emeralds, sapphire gleam.
Mysteries on wings drift by,
Silent songs, a timeless theme.

Beneath the arc where starlight spills,
Hues of twilight gently meld.
Nature wraps her nightly thrills,
In the magic, hearts upheld.

Moonlit paths where wishes tread,
Fluttering leaves and rustling grass.
In this realm where dreams are bred,
Time stands still, like fleeting glass.

Close your eyes and feel the art,
Lush hues weave through time and space.
In the night, the world's a heart,
Embracing each celestial trace.

## Curious Greenery Amongst the Mystic Shadows

Amidst the shade of ancient trees,
Curious sights catch wandering eyes.
Whispers rustle on the breeze,
As secrets dwell where magic lies.

Fern and ivy, entwined in plot,
Echoes of laughter, softly found.
In every corner, dreams begot,
Rustling tales spin around.

Mossy carpets, soft as sighs,
Crusted bark, a textured tale.
Here, creativity complies,
In shadows deep, the spirits sail.

Woven light through shifting leaves,
Eager hearts seek what's concealed.
Life reveals, and then deceives,
In this realm, all truth's revealed.

Curious minds, with wonder glowed,
Step by step, through whispered scenes.
Letting nature's magic goad,
Infusing life with vibrant greens.

## Vivid Strokes of Nature's Brush


With each dawn, the palette swells,
A symphony of tones anew.
Nature's canvas, where magic dwells,
Each stroke paints life's vibrant hue.

Golden rays on tranquil streams,
Bathe the world in amber light.
Every splash ignites our dreams,
In the shades of day and night.

Petals burst with fearless grace,
A riot of colors, bold and bright.
In nature's heart, we find our place,
Feeling the thrill of pure delight.

Brush the canvas with your soul,
Let the colors blend and sway.
In the wild, make yourself whole,
In vivid strokes, lose your way.

For life's a masterpiece, they say,
An ever-changing work of art.
Under sun or moonlight's play,
Nature beckons, play your part.

## Whispers of Enchanted Whimsy

In the hush where breezes sigh,
Dreams take flight and shadows lie.
Murmurs of the night unfold,
Secrets shimmer, stories told.

In a garden, wild and free,
Fairy lights dance joyfully.
Petals whisper ancient spells,
Carried by soft, tinkling bells.

Beneath the moon's gentle gaze,
Fanciful creatures weave their ways.
In every rustle, magic sings,
Awakening the world of things.

Cloaked in shimmering twilight haze,
Wandering through mysterious ways.
A tapestry of dreams entwined,
In the realm where hope is blind.

Together we shall chase the night,
Guided by the starry light.
With every step, a tale we weave,
In whispers of what we believe.

# Gleaming Strands of Arcane Light

In the depths where shadows dwell,
Spirits rise, enchanted well.
Threads of gold in twilight spun,
Magic twinkles, dreams begun.

With a flick and gentle sweep,
Wonders wake from slumber deep.
Illuminated paths align,
Destinies in starlight shine.

Whirling dust, a mystic dance,
Through the ages, lost in trance.
A tapestry, the cosmos sewn,
In the heart where magic's grown.

Gleaming strands of whispered lore,
Every heartbeat, tales explore.
Let the winds of fate be kind,
As we wander, hearts aligned.

Underneath the moonlit dome,
We seek the charm of ancient home.
Every spark ignites the night,
In this realm of arcane light.

## The Sorcerer's Flamboyant Threads

In a realm where colors blend,
Flamboyant threads the sorcerers send.
Each stitch a spell, a playful tease,
Weaving fate with elegant ease.

Casting colors with a sigh,
A rainbow's tale begins to fly.
Scarlet whispers, azure dreams,
In every yard of magic schemes.

Twisting patterns that delight,
In shadows cast by candlelight.
With every twist, enchantments bloom,
Filling spaces, banishing gloom.

Oh, how the fabrics swirl and dance,
Every thread, an ancient chance.
With joyful hands, they shape the night,
In flamboyant threads of pure delight.

Together we shall sew and rhyme,
Embroidering the threads of time.
With laughter woven in each seam,
We create our vibrant dream.

# A Symphony of Magical Frays

In the echo of twilight's call,
A symphony begins to fall.
Notes like whispers in the breeze,
Drifting softly through the trees.

With every chord, the magic swells,
Dancing through the secret knells.
Harmonies of the night ignite,
As starlit dreams take glowing flight.

Frayed edges of the universe,
A melody, a gentle curse.
Strings of fate entwined, they show,
In the shadows, secrets grow.

The conductor of this mystic night,
Guides us to the realms of light.
Together we shall sing and sway,
In a symphony of magical frays.

So let us raise our voices high,
Beneath the vast and endless sky.
With every note, our spirits soar,
Creating magic evermore.

# Bewitched Fibers of the Fabled Glade

In shadows deep, where whispers weave,
Bewitched fibers rise, the heart believes.
Draped in moss and secrets tight,
They shimmer softly in the moonlight.

A tapestry of dreams unfolds,
With stories ancient, tales retold.
Each strand a magic, spun with care,
In glade so fabled, spirits dare.

The silken threads of night and day,
Entwine the lost, the longing stay.
In every hue, a laughter rings,
Echoes of time, of forgotten things.

In this enchanted, hidden space,
Nature dances with gentle grace.
Bewitched fibers tell the lore,
Of wandering souls who seek for more.

With every flicker, every glance,
The fibers weave a timeless dance.
Through winds that whisper tales of old,
A magic waits, a realm of gold.

## Illuminous Wands of Tangle and Twirl

In hands so small, with dreams so grand,
Illuminous wands, crafted by hand.
They sparkle bright with unseen might,
In shadows deep, they bring the light.

Tangled in vines, adorned with stars,
Wands spin tales of the moon and Mars.
With every twirl, they sing a song,
A melody where all belong.

The flick of a wrist, a delicate trace,
Brings forth magic, a bright embrace.
In tangled realms where wishes bloom,
With wands that dance, they chase the gloom.

Each wand a story, each spark a dream,
In swirling clouds, they twist and beam.
With hearts aglow, they weave their spell,
In shadows deep, where magic dwells.

Through the air, their whispers fly,
In twinkling bits, they touch the sky.
Illuminous wands, so wild and free,
Unlock the bounds of mystery.

# Dance of Sorcery amidst Glimmering Crowns

In twilight's grace, the sorcery flows,
A dance of shadows, where enchantment grows.
Glimmering crowns atop the head,
Of those who dream, of magic bred.

With twirling robes and laughter bright,
They conjure wonders, day and night.
In every twirl, a secret spun,
In every laugh, a world begun.

Glimmers of gold and threads of fate,
In this grand dance, don't hesitate.
With every beat, the magic sways,
In rhythm set, in timeless ways.

The crowns they wear, a shining mark,
Of battles fought, of journeys sparked.
In swirling beauty, they take their flight,
A dance of sorcery, pure delight.

As starlight twinkles in the air,
The sorcerers revel, free from care.
With glowing crowns, they rise anew,
In every dance, a magic true.

# Curls of Gold in Fantastical Dusk

In dusk's embrace, the world transforms,
Curls of gold in gentle swarms.
Glimpses of sunlight, a fleeting kiss,
In magical moments, endless bliss.

With laughter bright, and spirits high,
The curls of gold cascade and fly.
They twirl in harmony with the breeze,
A symphony composed with ease.

In twilight gardens, where dreams awake,
Golden strands of joy, by shadows break.
Every curl whispers songs of old,
In this fantastical dusk of gold.

Through wandering fields, the magic sways,
In twilight's heart, where wonder lays.
With every sparkle, dazzling bright,
Curls of gold dance into the night.

In every flicker, every gleam,
These golden curls weave tales of dreams.
In fantastical dusk, they weave and spin,
Echoing the magic that lies within.

# Kaleidoscopic Hues in Nature's Embrace

In twilight's glow, colors blend,
Whispers of dusk, where shadows send.
Petals dance in the breeze's song,
Nature's canvas, vibrant and strong.

Crimson and gold in the fading light,
A tapestry woven, pure delight.
Each hue a tale, a secret shared,
In the heart of the forest, none unprepared.

With gentle caress, the sun dips low,
A painter's skill in every flow.
Leaves flutter softly, a soft parade,
In nature's embrace, memories unmade.

The river reflects the dying rays,
Sparkling jewels in the fading haze.
Every moment a magical weave,
In kaleidoscopic hues, we believe.

Sleep now, dear child, while the night sings,
Wrapped in the comfort that daylight brings.
Dream of colors, of life's sweet art,
In nature's embrace, we find our heart.

# Whirling Leaves in Spaces Beyond Time

In the autumn's breath, they twirl and soar,
Whirling leaves whisper tales of yore.
Each gust of wind, a gentle push,
Through time's embrace, they softly rush.

Golden-brown spirals, a sight to behold,
Kissing the ground as stories unfold.
In the symphony of a fading year,
Echoes of laughter draw ever near.

Floating down paths, where memories weave,
Underfoot treasures, we won't believe.
In the spaces beyond time they dance,
Inviting us all to take a glance.

With each twirl, a secret set free,
Of bygone summers and dreams to be.
Round and round, they swirl in delight,
In the winter's hush, they'll take flight.

So gather your heart in the autumn's song,
In nature's rhythm, you truly belong.
Through spaces and ages, forever roam,
With whirling leaves, we find our home.

# Mystic Greens in the Etchings of Dreams

In the silence of woods, where shadows sleep,
Mystic greens in the secrets we keep.
Ferns unfurl with a delicate grace,
A whisper of magic in this hidden space.

Moonlight glistens on emerald leaves,
Telling of wonders that nature weaves.
In dreams we wander, through glades so deep,
Where ancient spirits in silence creep.

The gentle rustle, a serenade sweet,
With every heartbeat, the earth's soft beat.
Mystical hues beneath starlit beams,
Paint the landscape of our wildest dreams.

Vines entwine in an emerald embrace,
Softly entwining the heart of the place.
In the realm of the night, the spirits rejoice,
In mystic greens, we find our voice.

So linger a moment, let wonders unfold,
In the etchings of dreams, be brave, be bold.
For the world holds secrets, both ancient and new,
In the mystic greens, find the magic in you.

# Vivid Echoes Beneath a Sorcerer's Hand


In the twilight air, where spells are cast,
Vivid echoes dance, shadows are vast.
With flickering lights in the twilight breeze,
Whispers of magic drift through the trees.

A sorcerer's touch paints the world bright,
Colors shimmering in the dimming light.
Each incantation, a thread in the weave,
Crafting a story that few can believe.

Beneath the moon, where enchantments blend,
Vivid echoes call, the night to transcend.
With secret sigils that twinkle and gleam,
Reality bends beneath the dream.

Glimmers of stardust, stories untold,
In the heart of the woods, the mysteries unfold.
With a wand and a whisper, the night expands,
Creating a cosmos in a sorcerer's hands.

So close your eyes and let visions flow,
In vivid echoes, let imagination grow.
For beneath the stars, in the night's soft hand,
Magic awaits, where we take our stand.